The Delft Belting International Simulation is based upon a real international Mergers and Acquisition (M&A) transaction. It involved a multi- billion dollar acquirer seeking to expand for the first time internationally.

The simulation allows participants to experience the whole M&A process for themselves – including triumphs and setbacks.

Introduction: Aims and purpose of the simulation

Background: Setting the context of the deal

Your position

Getting started: Key considerations as the simulation commences

Appendices: *Indicative Timetable*

Group and Individual Assessments

Selected readings

Lecture slides

Introduction

Mergers and Acquisitions (M&A) are a long -lived, major global business phenomena involving trillions of dollars annually. Collectively they affect global trade flows, national economies, regional development, industries, organisations, competitors, business units, customers, suppliers, partners, owners, employees and other stakeholders (Angwin, 2007).

A simulation of an acquisition is very useful for the integration module of an MBA or MSc as it involves consideration of all the disciplines studied during the programme. For instance strategy and economics often underlie explanation for why acquisitions take place, finance theories inform valuation, marketing focuses upon customer impact, operations management, organisational behaviour and design theories give insight into how merging businesses and employees may work together, and psychology shows how living through such deals impacts upon individuals.. 'This module is complemented by the first multi-disciplinary text on M&A, 'Mergers and Acquisitions', Angwin (2007) published by Wiley.

This integration course will begin with a brief review of M&A strategy and process and then participants will be taken through a simulation of a real cross-border acquisition. As the simulation unfolds, participants will be able to draw upon all their learning from the MBA/MSc programme, to help them interpret and act as they attempt in competing teams to negotiate a successful deal. Comparison then will be made with what actually happened in the real world.

Aims and Purpose

General aims

1. To **integrate** MBA/MSc programme modules
   a. To complete the simulation effectively participants need to draw on **all the knowledge** they acquired during their MBA programme
      i. omitting areas of knowledge are likely to harmful to acquisition performance as purchasing a company requires a comprehensive understanding of **all aspects of the business**, not just legal and financial issues.
2. To **test** the ability of participant teams to **search** for relevant data and so more closely approximate reality than a conventional case study.
   a. Unlike conventional case studies, where material is neatly packaged and handed out for participants to analyse, here participant teams have to direct their own investigations: to search for relevant information, evaluate its quality and **'create'** their own dataset to analyse.
   b. The simulation tests participants searching abilities (not tested by other programmes), their analytical skills (including how much they have absorbed from their degree programme), and their reflective skills that allow feedback into their search processes.
   c. A unique feature of the simulation is that teams create their own pathway through the material so no two outcomes are the same.
3. To **engage** participants in multiple levels of communication skills
   a. Participants will have to work with a range of stakeholders requiring very different forms of negotiation

Mergers and Acquisition specific aims

1. Introduce participants to M&A strategies, motives, processes, and terminology.
2. To understand a range of M&A strategic options
3. To engage in and understand the M&A due diligence process
4. To apply M&A valuation techniques
5. To engage in deal negotiation
6. To understand key strategic elements in a M&A contract
7. To realise the importance of post-acquisition integration
8. To understand final deal outcomes based upon the overall M&A process.

Background

The simulation is based on a real transaction I conducted whilst working as a senior investment banker based in the UK subsidiary of the world's largest bank in London, UK. Every effort has been made to preserve the integrity of this information throughout the simulation, although the actual identities of the companies are disguised.

In 19x3 a large private Japanese corporation, Mega Industries, was intent on moving into Europe by acquiring an industrial belt manufacturing company in Holland, Delft Belting International, in order to access European markets.

Delft Belting International BV was a privately owned company located in the town of Delft in Holland (the Netherlands). It manufactured high quality automotive belting for many of Europe's leading car companies. Mega Industries ordered some of Delft Belting International's product some years previously in order to help it fulfil an order obligation for a Japanese client and was very pleased with its quality – indeed it was superior to its own automotive belt.

As Mega Industries had no prior experience of internationalising, as all their expansion to date had been within the highly competitive Japanese market. They also had no prior experience of making acquisitions, so they were entirely reliant on the advice of their financial advisor, the world's largest bank at the time, who owned a merchant bank in London with significant experience of international corporate finance. The reliance of

Mega Industries upon the London based merchant bank gave the corporate finance team in London a complete overview of the entire deal from beginning to end, and a very high degree of control over the entire process.

Your position

- The simulation casts you and your team as a recently hired M&A department of a London Merchant Bank, recently acquired by a Japanese International Bank. Your London bank's business largely consists of corporate finance (M&A and other corporate advisory work), leasing, some commercial and private banking and a small amount of equity and currency market dealing.

- It is the direct responsibility of your M&A team to achieve a successful deal for your client, the large Japanese corporation, Mega Industries. Due to the 'hands-off' position adopted by your client, as they have no prior experience of M&A, you are acting as 'principal' in this deal and need to take the initiative in all relevant matters. Success or failure in this deal is almost entirely down to your efforts.

- At the beginning of the simulation the class will be split into several competing banks. Each M&A team will represent a different advisory bank – there are other banks and companies that want to acquire Delft Belting International. All will be in direct competition. This 'contested' bid situation means that there will be several competing bids, but only one bid can win.

Getting Started

The course will begin with two or three introductory lectures, Part 1 (see indicative timetable on page 16), depending upon whether the class has already received a course on M&A. The class will be divided into different groups.

Selecting Bosses

Bosses are key to successful running of the simulation as they are the interface between the professor(s) and the class. Depending on class size,

between 1 and 3 bosses will be selected. To be a Boss the individual should be comfortable with basic financial calculations, as one would expect from a boss in a bank, but it is not necessary, and perhaps even undesirable for the Boss to be an M&A expert, as their history has been one of progression through commercial banking. In other words, the Boss is competent to understand team financial calculations, but is not able to give technical advice about transacting the M&A deal – this is why the M&A teams were hired.

Each boss can manage up to 3 teams. These bosses will be the Executive Directors in the London based subsidiary (see Your Location in the Bank p12). They will be responsible for several competing banks in order to illustrate how they would have many projects to oversee, and so cannot focus on just one team. The bosses hired their M&A teams in order to transact this specific deal, as they are not expert themselves.

The big advantage of playing a Boss in this simulation is that you will have a global view of the whole M&A process. In liaising with the Professors throughout the simulation you will have a privileged position in being able to see how your teams are evaluated and the issues that the Professors focus upon as critical to deal success – an objectivity that competing teams cannot have. The Bosses will present their own views of the M&A process to the class at the end of the module and this generally reveals an important dimension to the simulation that team members would not be able to perceive otherwise.

Selecting competing teams

Once the bosses have been selected, the class will then be divided into

competing teams of advisory banks (see 'Your location in the Bank' p12). The optimal size of a bank is between 6 and 8 participants. These teams then need to choose two observers (only one observer if the team size is between 5 and 6 members).

The remaining team members constitute the 'competing bank' and will work to transact the acquisition of Delft Belting. Their aim is to negotiate the best deal for their client, Mega Industries. However there are many banks trying to do the deal, and there can only be one owner.

The advantages of the role is that the team members will experience first-hand all the struggles, frustrations and successes of trying to research, negotiate and complete the acquisition of Delft Belting. Teams will own their results entirely and from the overall outcomes will be able to directly assess those things they did well and those things that might be improved in future. Every team will have to present their deal results to their client at the end of the simulation.

Selecting Observers

Each Bank needs to select two observers (only one observer if the team size is between 5 and 6 members). These observers shall watch their team as it works its way through the acquisition process, and record information about how they approached this activity. The  Professor(s) will give detailed guidance on how this is to be done. In particular Observers will collect data that can be analysed to show the different ways in which their team tackles a very complex problem. Together with the other observers in other teams, all of the data collected will be analysed and synthesized in order to fully understand each of the banks' approaches to the acquisition challenge. These results will be fed back to the whole class at the end of the module in order that everyone can understand the most effective ways in which to transact M&A.

Observers can only observe their own team, and they are not allowed to sit in on other competing groups, to protect group confidentiality.

The benefits of the observer role is that you will be able to see the whole M&A process objectively and perceive what things work effectively and those that do not. The feedback that Observers provide to the class at the end of the simulation is perhaps the most valuable insight from the whole exercise.

Your location in the bank

The Figure below shows the location of the corporate finance team and its boss in the London subsidiary of the world's largest bank (see red typing). The boss is the Executive Director responsible for Europe, Middle East and Africa, with emphasis on corporate finance, some commercial banking and leasing.

Boss and Bank Subsidiary Location

The relationship with Mega Industries, your client, is held by the major corporate clients department in Tokyo. You cannot communicate effectively with that department or the client as you are not sufficiently senior in your organisation. Therefore you need to communicate through your boss for information from those sources. Specifically you will need to write down any questions and requests of your client and submit this to your Boss for approval and for submission to Head Office. Failure to follow this approach will result in either a dismissive response or no response at all from Head Office. You will not make any friends at all if you try contacting the client directly, as this will be perceived as undermining the authority of your Boss and your London based CEO.

General Comments

- The Simulation will start with Competing Banks being issued with **Information Sheet 1** and tasked with creating a strategy statement for their bank in order to establish their identity. Teams will be briefed on how to do this in class.

- Competing Banks shall then follow an acquisition process. An idealised process is summarised on page 15 following this section. The

simulation works on the issuance of a series of **Information Sheets** at critical moments throughout the M&A process. These sheets will inform competing banks on the scope and limits to their activities at each stage.

- Bosses and Observers will meet with the Professor(s) for a detailed briefing on their activities once the lectures are finished. Once these briefings are done, the active 'lecturing' part of the module is finished and the Professor(s) cease to be Professors unless specifically requested. They will now take on the identities of other key actors in the Simulation. The teams should now think of themselves as competing banks and should act as such.

- Eavesdropping should be resisted as other groups may well be following 'red herrings' and either wittingly trying, or unwittingly, to mislead you. However, should anything be overheard, unlike a classroom situation where you might be accused of cheating, in the simulation this is put down to industrial espionage. You must protect the confidentiality of your client's and your own information.

- Competing Banks must assume that the Professors are no longer 'the professors' but that one is Mr van Meerden, the owner of The Dutch Belting International B.V.. Depending upon how many Professors are involved in the simulation, other roles they play include the Head of the Bank's Credit Committee, Mr Oosterhouse, the Marketing and

Sales Director of Delft Belting International B.V., Mrs Witt, Chief Engineer of Delft Belting International B.V., a major customer of the company. Should any bank wish to speak to a Professor, as Professor, then they must request this specifically, or the answer they shall receive will be from Mr Van Meerden.

Good luck!

The Acquisition Process

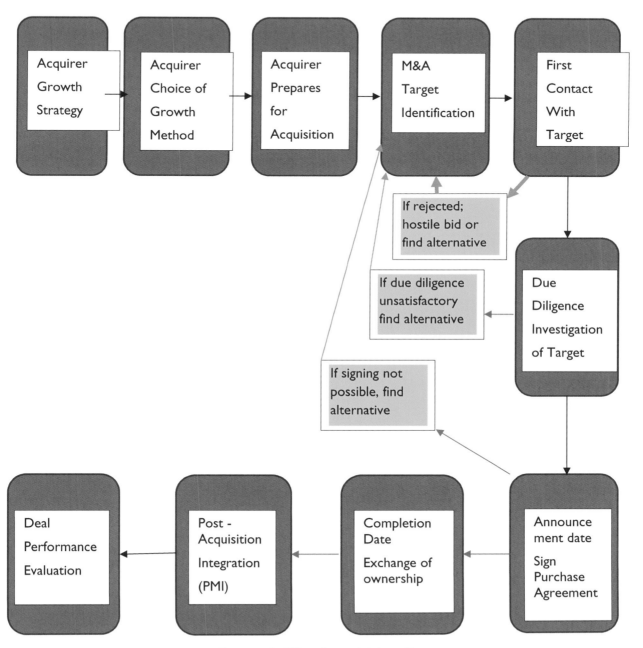

Figure 1: The Acquisition Process

© Duncan Angwin, 2018

Appendices

Indicative Timetable

Part 1: Opening lectures:

- The world of M&A
- M&A Advisors

Part 2: The Delft Belting Simulation:

- Introduction
- Organising into teams

Part 3: Getting going:

- Bank activity: Design Strategy Statement
- Receive Information Sheet 1
- Observer and Boss preparation

Part 4: The main simulation:

- Delft Belting Press Conference
- Banks to complete internal 'Bid Document'
- Banks to conduct due diligence and negotiations
- Banks to negotiate and finalise Contracts
- Banks to present deal to clients

Part 5: Post simulation wrap up:

- Observers and bosses present analysis
- 'What actually happened

Assessments

Group Assessment

40% indicative score

Groups are:

1. Competing banks 2. Boss group 3. Observers group

Submission:

1 pdf document of all the materials produced during the simulation

1. Bank Group Assessment Documentation

Front page, identifying the all bank members – please identify the Boss and Observers clearly.

1. **Bank profile statement** [Mission, vision, values]
2. **Bid document** [Internal bank document: deal strategy; valuation; negotiation approach; main due diligence items]
3. **Final contract, signed.**
4. **Press release.**
5. **Client presentation.**

Hand written is OK – but these should be scanned in so they can be included in the PDF.

No further text is required.

2. <u>Boss Group</u> Assessment Documentation

Front page, identifying the all bank members – please identify the team and the observer(s) clearly.

1. Boss presentation slides

No further text is required.

3. <u>Observer Group</u> Assessment Documentation

Front page, identifying the all bank members – please identify the Boss and your team clearly.

1. Observer presentation slides

No further text is required.

Individual Assessment

60% indicative score

- **Assessment for <u>Bank Group Individuals</u>**

- **2 pages only**

- **Page 1**

    - Individual's name (Group membership i.e. Bank; Boss; Observer)

    - Deal summary table (see figure below)

        - Your deal compared with another deal or 'ideal' deal. Final column will show gaps.

        - You identify key variables for comparison

    - No other text is required

Deal elements (you need to identify these) ↓	Your Bank's actual deal	'Ideal' deal (another bank's deal, or remembered from final class discussion)	Performance gaps (good and bad)
Upfront price			
Deferred consideration			
…			
…			

- **Page 2**

- **Statement of Reflections and Learning (<u>1 page maximum</u>)**
    - Drawing upon your analysis of your table on page 1 – <u>**explain the differences in performance**</u> between your bank's deal and the 'ideal' deal.
    - Using information provided by the Observers and the Bosses in their presentation<u>**, identify the main learning points**</u> from the simulation. There may be areas where their insights give you fresh understanding, or there may be areas where their perspectives and yours are quite different.

- Your own reflections on the simulation should include:
    - a critical appraisal of how this 'real world' simulation matches up with the theory that you have learnt from your various courses.
    - a review of how you and your team have 'problem solved' in the face of incomplete information, inaccurate or non-verifiable information, time pressure, process problems, organisational and cultural differences, logistical challenges.
    - If you were now to conduct an acquisition in real life – what would be the key things you would want to get right? What are the 'takeaways'?

Assessment for <u>Boss and Observer Group</u>

<u>Individuals</u>

- **2 pages only**

- **Page 1**

  - Individual's name (Group membership i.e. Bank; Boss; Observer)

  - Produce a summary set of your groups findings as a table or figure (you may already have a concluding slide you can use from the group presentation)

  - No other text is required

- **Page 2**

- **Statement of Reflections and Learning (<u>1 page maximum</u>)**
  - Reflect upon the conclusions of your presentation now that you have experienced the final outcomes of the simulation.
  - Identify **<u>the main learning points</u>** from the simulation.

- Your own reflections on the simulation should include:
  - a critical appraisal of how this 'real world' simulation matches up with the theory that you have learnt from your various courses.

  - a review of how the teams 'problem solved' in the face of incomplete information, inaccurate or non-verifiable information, time pressure, process problems, organisational and cultural differences, logistical challenges.

  - If you were now to conduct an acquisition in real life – what would be the key things you would want to get right? What are the 'takeaways'?

Selected M&A references

Text Book

Angwin, D.N. (2007) *Mergers and Acquisitions*. Published by Blackwell Publishing, Wiley, Oxford. ISBN 978-1-4051-224

Other M&A Books

Angwin, D. N. (2000) *Implementing Successful Post-Acquisition Management*, Senior Executive Briefing. Financial Times Management Series/Prentice Hall.

DePamphlis, D. M. (2008). *Mergers, Acquisitions and Other Restructuring Activities*, 4th edition. Burlington, MA: Academic Press, Elsevier.

Faulkner, D. and Teerikangas, S., (2012). *The Oxford Handbook of Mergers and Acquisitions*. Oxford: Oxford University Press.

Sudarsanam, S. (2010) *Creating Value from Mergers and Acquisitions: The Challenges*, 2nd edition. FT Prentice Hall.

Journal articles

Angwin, D. N., Paroutis, S. and Connell, R. (2015) Why Good Things Don't Happen: The Micro-foundations of Routines in the M&A Process, *Journal of Business Research*.

Angwin, D.N., Mellahi, K. Gomes, E., Peters, E. (2014) How communication approaches impact mergers and acquisitions outcomes, *International Journal of Human Resource Management* http://dx.doi.org/10.1080/09585192.2014.985330.

Angwin, D. N. and Urs, U. (2014) The effect of routine aggregations in post merger integration performance: whether to 'combine' or 'superimpose' for synergy gains? *Advances in Mergers and Acquisitions*, JAI Press, 13:153-179.

Angwin, D. N. and Meadows, M. (2014) New integration strategies for post-acquisition management, *Long Range Planning* (available on-line May 2014). DOI: 10.1016/j.lrp.2014.04.001.

Angwin, D. N. and Meadows, M. (2013) Acquiring poorly performing companies during economic recession: Insights into post-acquisition management. *Journal of General Management* 38 (1): 1-24. Autumn.

Angwin, D. N., Gomes, E., Weber, Y., Tarba, S. (2013) Critical success factors through the Mergers and Acquisitions process: revealing pre- and post-M&A connections for improved performance, *Thunderbird International Business Review*, Wiley, 55 (1): 13-35 Jan-Feb.

Angwin, D.N., Gomes, E., Melahi, K. (2012) HRM practices throughout the Mergers and Acquisition (M&A) Process: A study of domestic deals in the Nigerian Banking Industry, *International Journal of Human Resource Management*, 23 (14): 2874 -2900.

Angwin, D. N. (2006) Motive Architypes In Mergers and Acquisitions (M&A): The Implications Of A Configurational Approach To Performance, *Strategic Management Conference,* Vienna.

Angwin, D. N., Stern, P. and Bradley, S. (2004) Agent or Steward: the target CEO in a hostile takeover: can a condemned agent be redeemed?', Long Range Planning, 37, Elsevier: 239-257 Angwin, D. N. (2003) Strategy as Exploration and Interconnection, chapter 8 in Wilson,D.C. and Cummings, S.C. (eds) *Images of Strategy*, Blackwells, Oxford.

Angwin, D. N. and Savill, B. (1997) Strategic perspectives on European cross-border acquisitions -- a view from top European executives, *European Management Journal*, vol. 15, no. pp. 423—35

Bower, J. L. (2004) Not all M&As are alike and that matters, *Harvard Business Review*, 79, 3: 93-101

Bruner, R. F. (2002) Does M&A pay? A survey of evidence for the decision maker, *Journal of Applied Finance*, 12,1: 48-68.

Buono, A. F. and Bowditch, J. L. (1989) *The Human Side of Mergers and Acquisitions: Managing Collisions Between People and Organizations.* San Francisco: Jossey-Bass.

Haleblian, J., Devers, C. E., McNamara, G., Carpenter, M. A. and Davison, R. B., 2009. Taking Stock of What We Know About Mergers and Acquisitions: A Review and Research Agenda. *Journal of Management,* 35, 3, 469-502.

Haspeslagh, P. C. and Jemison, D. B. (1991) *Managing Acquisitions*. New York: The Free Press.

Hassett, M., E., Vincze, Z., Urs, U., Angwin, D.N., Nummela, N., Zettinig, P. (2016) Cross-border mergers and acquisitions from India – Motives and integration strategies of Indian acquirers, in Value Creation in International Business. Palgrave Macmillan ISBN: 9783319308029. Electronic ISBN: 9783319308036

Hayward, M. L. A. and Hambrick, D. C. (1997) Explaining the premium paid for large acquisitions: evidence of CEO hubris, *Administrative Science Quarterly*, 42, 1: 103-129

Jensen, M. and Meckling, W. (1976) Theory of the firm: managerial behaviour, agency costs, and owner- ship structure, *Journal of Financial Economics*, vol. 3, pp. 305--60.

Meglio, O. and Risberg, A., (2010) Mergers and acquisitions - Time for a methodological rejuvenation of the field? *Scandinavian Journal of Management*, 26, 1, 87–95.

Mirvis, P. H. and Marks, M. L. (1992) *Managing the Merger: Making it Work*. Englewood Cliffs, NJ: Prentice Hall.

Muehlfeld, K., Rao Sahib, P., & Witteloostuijn, A.v. (2012). A contextual theory of organizational learning from failures and successes – A study of acquisition completion in the global newspaper industry, 1981-2008. *Strategic Management Journal*, **33**, 938-64.

Puranam, P., Singh, H., & Chaudhuri, S. (2009). Integrating acquired capabilities: When structural integration is (un)necessary. *Organization Science*, 20, 313-328.

Puranam, P. and Srikanth, K., (2007). What they know vs. what they do: how acquirers leverage technology acquisitions, *Strategic Management Journal*, 28, 805-825.

Ranft, A.L., Lord, M.D., (2000), Acquiring new knowledge: the role of retaining human capital in acquisitions of high-tech firms, *Journal of High Tech. Manage. Res.*: 295–319.

Roll, R. (1986) The hubris hypothesis of corporate takeovers, *Journal of Business*, 59: 197-216.

Rouzies, A., Coleman, H., Angwin, D. N. (2018) Distorted and Adaptive Integration: realized post-acquisition integration as embedded in an ecology of processes, *Long Range Planning*. https://doi.org/10.1016/j.lrp.2018.03.003

Trautwein, F. (1990) Merger motives and merger prescriptions, *Strategic Management Journal*, 11: 283–95.

Wernerfelt, B. (1984) A resource based view of the firm, *Strategic Management Journal*, 5 (2): 171-180.

Yakis-Douglas, B., Angwin, D.N., Ahn, K., Meadows, M. (2016) Opening M&A strategy to investors: Predictors and outcomes of transparency during organizational transition, <u>*Long Range Planning*</u>, available on line. http://dx.doi.org/10.1016/j.lrp.2016.06.007.

Zaheer, A., Castaner, X. and Souder, D., 2013. Synergy Sources, Target Autonomy, and Integration in Acquisitions, *Journal of Management*, 39, 604-632. March

Zollo, M. and Singh, H., 2004. Deliberate Learning in corporate acquisitions: post-acquisition strategies and integration capability in U.S. Bank mergers, *Strategic Management Journal*, 25: 1233-1256.

Lecture Slides

Delft Belting
M&A Context

by
Professor Duncan Angwin

Introduction

- My background and experience in M&A
  - Rolls Royce v. Kit Car deals
- Your experience
  - What is important?
    - What works
    - What goes wrong
- Session Structure
  - Summary of M&A lecture
  - Lecture by Associate Professor on M&A in practice
  - Introduction to the role of the adviser
  - Introduction to Delft Belting Simulation

Prof Duncan Angwin *Slide 2*

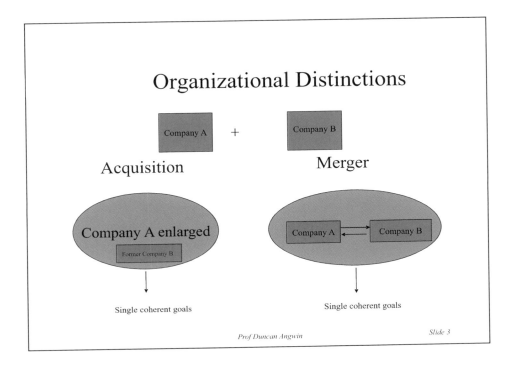

Organizational Distinctions

Company A + Company B

Acquisition   Merger

Company A enlarged

Former Company B

Company A ⇄ Company B

Single coherent goals   Single coherent goals

Prof Duncan Angwin   *Slide 3*

Some M&A definitions

- Acquisitions
  - The purchase of one firm by another => enlarged acquirer
  - Frequently the acquirer is larger than the target
    - Exceptions
      - Reverse takeover
      - Leveraged finance – Hoylake v. BAT: £15bn!
  - Main approaches/styles
    - *Friendly:* receives approval of target company management
    - *Hostile*: target management doesn't approve of offer to shareholders
- Merger
  - A new firm created out of original firms
  - 'Equals' - similar sized firms where none dominate
- Language distinction blurred in practice

Prof Duncan Angwin   *Slide 4*

Benefits of M&A

- Combining two firms through M&A must result in
  1. A greater value than the two firms on their own
  2. A greater value than the two firms working together in another way i.e. through contract/joint venture etc
  - When do parent companies prefer M&A over other growth methods?
- This 'extra' value is often termed 'synergies'
  - Resources and capabilities (human and technological)
- The problem with 'synergies' it that they are illusive – promising great gains but understate the costs of realising them.

Prof Duncan Angwin   *Slide 5*

AOL / Time Warner:
the mother of all mergers

- *When Steve Case..[hugged] Jerry Levin on stage as they announced their epic deal, it was a rare show of emotion*
- *For once the hype seemed justified. The $150bn takeover of Time Warner by America Online is not just another record breaking deal. It is one of those events that have the potential to change the competitive landscape so fundamentally that nothing can be the same again.*

Source: The Economist January 13, 2000

- Cartoon of the time showed a giant AOL/Time Warner Space ship threatening an American consumer with 'You've got Mail!'

Prof Duncan Angwin *Slide 6*

Losing its magic

- *Only 6 months ago the merger of AOL and Time Warner was reshaping the media industry... Then the talk was all about harnessing the dynamism of the internet and the entrepreneurial spirit of the geeks from AOL... to revitalise the rather frumpy old-media assets of Time Warner. "Synergy" was the buzzword....*
- *Buy Time Warner and get an AOL for free!!*

In the 18 months following the merger, **AOL/Time Warner** capitalization fell from $250bn to $125bn; **Walt Disney** from $70bn to $45bn **Yahoo** from $120bn to $8bn

Prof Duncan Angwin   7

Global M&A activity

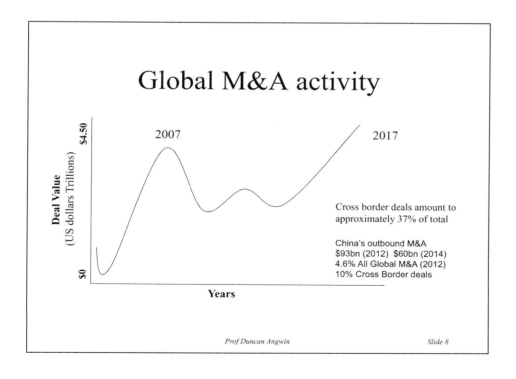

Deal Value (US dollars Trillions)

$4.50

2007   2017

Cross border deals amount to approximately 37% of total

China's outbound M&A $93bn (2012) $60bn (2014) 4.6% All Global M&A (2012) 10% Cross Border deals

$0

Years

Prof Duncan Angwin   *Slide 8*

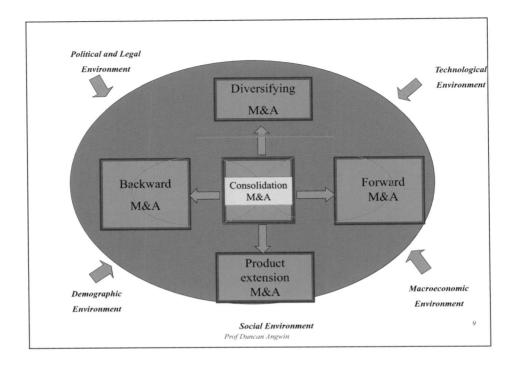

Prof Duncan Angwin

M&A as an effective response

- Changes in the macro-environment throws up challenges and opportunities
- M&A is an effective response to changes in
  - The macro environment (ESTEMPLE)
  - The competitive environment
- Also in anticipation of environmental changes/constraints

Prof Duncan Angwin   *Slide 10*

Six distinctive M&A strategies

Overcapacity	Eliminate capacity for market share and efficiency	Unigate Daimler-Chrysler
Geographic	Expand geographically	HSBC Tesco
Product	Extend product line Internationally	Quaker Oats and Snapple Nestle and Rowntree Kraft and Cadbury
R&D	Buying innovation rather than in-house	Cisco Systems Pfizer and Warner Lambert
Convergence	Betting on new industry emerging	AOL and Time Warner Google Glasses
Investment	A financial acquirer	Nomura and Greenalls Taverns Macquarie Bank Ltd (Aus) and Birmingham Airport Hldgs (24%)

Adapted from Bower, HBR, 2001   *Prof Duncan Angwin*   *Slide 11*

Advantages of acquisitions

(Warwick Business School / Ernst & Young survey of Cross-Border Acquisitions, 1996)

- **Speed: as competitive advantage**
    - in anticipation of opportunities or threats
    - *'its the only way of establishing an immediate position in the market place'*
- **Control: (50% JVs are unstable)**
    - *'You have total control and independence which you would not have if it were a joint venture for example'.*
- **Enrich core competencies/capabilities: learning**
- **Don't disturb competitive balance in mature industries**
- **Achieving scale and using resources**
- **High profile**

Prof Duncan Angwin   *Slide 12*

Disadvantages of acquisitions

- **Can be expensive - 30% - 50% premiums**
  - More expensive if hostile
  - City problem of walking away from a deal
- **Assumes suitable targets available**
- **High failure rate**
- **Can damage the parent**

Prof Duncan Angwin   *Slide 13*

Why do M&A under perform?

- McKinsey survey (2002)

  - 70% of mergers failed to achieve anticipated revenue synergies

  - Revenue dis-synergies often ignored

  - One quarter of companies overestimated cost synergies by at least 25%

  - One-time costs often underestimated

  - Errors about timing: cost savings take longer to materialise and are less sustainable

Prof Duncan Angwin   *Slide 14*

Summary

- M&A is an effective, speedy response to environmental change (real or anticipated)
- Can lead to sustained competitive advantage through capturing
  - defendable positions in markets/industries
  - scarce/unique/valuable resources
  - Creating new opportunities
- Can cause substantial value destruction
  - Overpayment
  - Over-optimism
  - Unrealised synergies
- 82% of top managers believe M&A to be successful. Consultants believe 83% fail (KPMG)!

Prof Duncan Angwin   *Slide 15*

Transacting*Mergers*and* Acquisitions

Merchant*Banks*5 a*dying*breed?

Prof*Duncan*Angwin

Merchant)banks)- A)dying)breed?

- Context
  - *Competitors*
  - *Major)environmental)changes*
- Merchant)bank)activities)
- What)makes)good)/)bad)clients?
- How)substantial)is)their)competitive) advantage?

Major environmental changes

- Rapid growth in securities market (vast profits), increased sophistication
- Last M&A wave in banking: Horizontal M&A →Universal Banks?
- Competing on Capital intensiveness;
  - scale economies - global; equipment;
  - scale of borrowing;
  - volume of investors;
  - move from competing on know-how and connections, to competing on cost and infra-structure;
  - capital adequacy

M & A Competitors

- Competitors
  - Merchant Banks, Investment banks, Boutiques, Stockbrokers, Commercial banks, Accountancy firms
- Own background - Investment / Merchant banks
- Investment banker
  - high tech., 'positive' attitude, telephone numbers, scale *(Salomons, Morgan Stanley, Merrill Lynch)*
- Merchant banker
  - long history, genteel sophistication, corridors of power, risk takers, small *(Rothschilds, Hambros, Lazards)*

Merchant Bank Scope

- Chinese Walls - some banks prefer not to have an equity arm to avoid problems

- Security remote access doors

  proofed windows (protect computers)

  secure car park

'Hermetically sealed from the bank'!

What make good or bad clients?

GOOD

- Big deal (fees 2%) Hoylake deal £13,000,000,000 =>£26m! => Prestige
- Single driving CEO or Chairman with clear objectives
  - On top of the deal and can make decisions quickly
- Trust their advisers, not too greedy and pay their bills!
- Come back with new deals - not complaints and law suits
- Straightforward deal with rights issue

BAD

- Multiple viewpoints (Babcock & Brown Money Brokers)
- Secret deals and shady issues (Illegal dealings, SFO, Knee cappers)
- Can't be controlled (George Walker)
- Too greedy, playing advisers off against each other, changing their minds (success fees)

What techniques are used in acquisition?

- 40% Legal issues

- 40% Accounting & Finance issues

- 20% Negotiation

Has changed over time- means peopled by different styles ->implications!

· Merchant Bank role

- Oversee deal - coordinate and control all aspects

- Produce offer document

- Drive deal forward - probably negotiate deal

- Ensure all necessary items are in place to ensure signing of contract

- In some ways, a surrogate CEO

'He is there to guide and protect and realise his fee'!

The Mergers & Acquisitions business

· How do you compete?

✎ **Spotting deals - Who are targets?**

- Market for Corporate Control: Poor management replaced

- Performance problems (environmental change)

- Good Management

- Synergies

- Exit strategies for investors, ageing owner

- A competitive threat (critic size in the computer industry)

✎ **Spotting deals - Who are the acquirers**

- Cash rich

- Acquisitive - need to grow, but strength or weakness?

- CEO ego

How do Banks compete?

❖ Innovative solutions — Financing, Private knowledge

❖ Quality of advice — Technical, Market 'saviness'

❖ Quality in process mgt — Efficient, Discrete, Handle authorities
   — actually getting the deal done!

❖ Style and personnalities — English roast dinner v. Paribas' Roux Bros

Answer :	*'Mystique' + dialogue*

❖ **What is your bank's identity?**

It can't happen to us!

➤ Adhesives company — Drops for dollars?

➤ Engineering company — But he drives a Range Rover!
   ➤ *relatedness may not be a protection*

➤ Gas Company — Interrupted payments?
   ➤ *different business practices across borders*

➤ Land company — We have the tax records!
   ➤ *codified knowledge is not always the most important knowledge*

➤ Pharmaceutical company — Three headquarters!and we can't sit down!
   ➤*The problems of superficial cultural interpretation*

Delft Belting Briefing
Process, Timetable and Assessment

Professor Duncan Angwin

Delft Belting Briefing

The Acquisition process

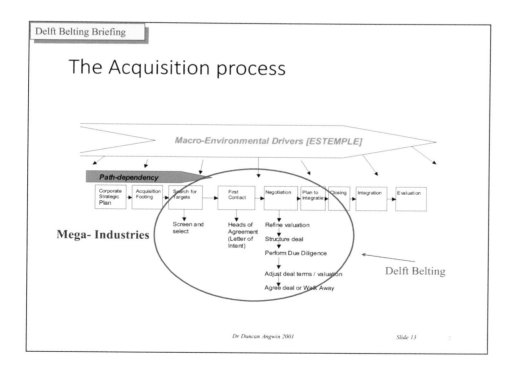

Mega- Industries

Delft Belting

Dr Duncan Angwin 2001   *Slide 13*

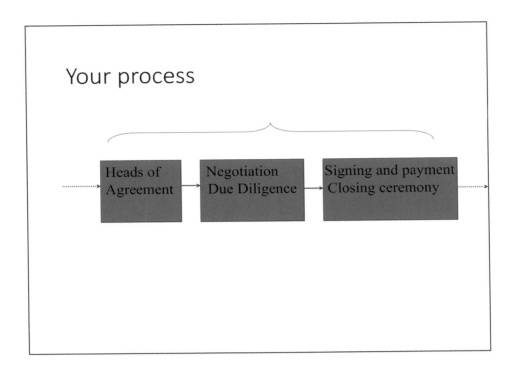

Your process

Heads of Agreement → Negotiation Due Diligence → Signing and payment Closing ceremony

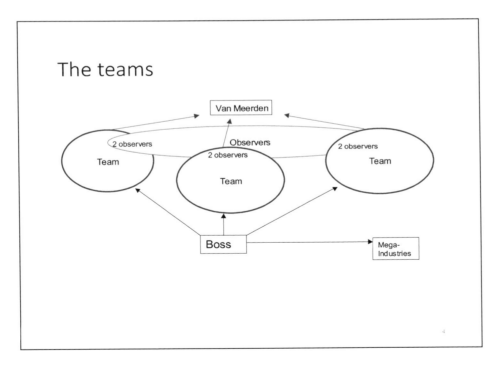

The teams

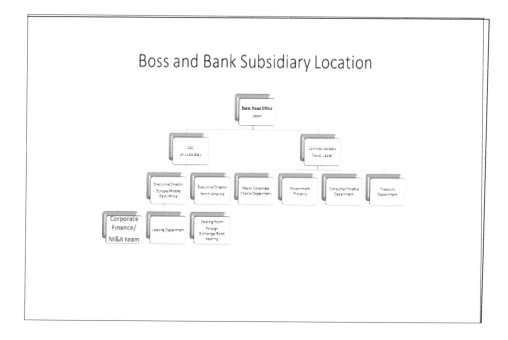

Boss and Bank Subsidiary Location

Delft Belting: Indicative 3 day timetable: Day 1

- Opening lectures [M&A context, Advisors, Delft Briefing]
  BREAK
- Group meetings
  - Select observers and bosses
  - Teams establish
    - Bank identity/name
      - Mission statement
      - Core values/style
      - Competitive advantage
    - Read participants manual
    - Prepare for Van Meerden press conference
  - Bosses meet for briefing in lecture theatre (Professor)
  - Observers meet for briefing in lecture theatre (Professor)
    LUNCH
- Van Meerden addresses the team
- Teams prepare a 'bid document'
  - internal justification
  - bid limits
  - negotiation strategy
- Bid document is reviewed by the boss.
  Bid document <u>has to be signed off</u> by boss before teams can progress!
  END

Delft Belting: Indicative Timetable: Day 2

- Once Bid Document is signed, Competing Banks can
    - - meet and negotiate with Van Meerden
    - - gather information from consultant reports
    - - draft contract
- Finalize contract
    - - The contract must be signed by all relevant parties!

        Lunch

- Teams prepare
    - presentation to Mega Industries
    - press release
- Observers and bosses prepare presentations

Delft Belting: Indicative Timetable: Day 3

- Bank groups present their deals to Mega-Industries

    Break

- Bosses presentation to the group
- Observers presentation to the group

    Lunch

- Subsequent events
    - Observers rejoin their teams
- Groups work on statement
    - Actual position of their bank
    - Actions taken/intended

    Break

- Groups present statement to the class for acceptance
- 'What actually happened'

Group Assessments

- **Groups are 1. Competing banks 2. Boss group 3. Observers group)**
- **Submission will be 1 pdf document of all the materials produced during the simulation**
- **Group (Bank) Assessment Documentation**
  - **Front page**, identifying the all bank members – please identify the Boss and Observers clearly.
  - **Bank profile statement** [Mission, vision, values]
  - **Bid document** [Internal bank document: deal strategy; valuation; negotiation approach]
  - **Final signed contract**
  - **Press release**
  - **Client presentation**
  - Hand written OK – but these should be scanned in so they can be included in the PDF.
- **Group (Boss) Assessment Documentation**
  - **Front page**, identifying the all bank members – please identify the team and the observer(s) clearly.
  - **Boss presentation slides**
- **Group (Observer) Assessment Documentation**
  - **Front page**, identifying the all bank members – please identify the Boss and your team clearly.
  - **Observer presentation slides**

Individual Assessment

- 2 pages
- **Page 1**
  - Individual's name (Group membership i.e. Bank; Boss; Observer)
  - Deal summary table
    - Your deal compared with another deal or 'ideal' deal. Final column will show gaps.
    - You identify key variables for comparison
  - No other text

Individual Assessment

- **Page 2**
- **Statement of Reflections and Learning (<u>1 page maximum</u>)**
  - Drawing upon your analysis of your table on page 1 – <u>**explain the differences in performance**</u> between your bank's deal and the 'ideal' deal.
  - Using information provided by the Observers and the Bosses in their presentation, <u>**identify the main learning points**</u> from the simulation.
  - If you were now to conduct an acquisition in real life – what would be the key things you would want to get right? What are the 'takeaways'?

11

Case philosophy

- Businesses are often faced with uncertainty
  - buying in Eastern Europe (post USSR), China
  - Buying new technology
- Methods and approaches needed are completely new
  - Need to think broadly and draw on all your skills from your MBA/MSc programme
- The Delft Belting Simulation is excellent for you to try out your search, selection, analysis, synthesis and reflective skills
- The Delft Belting Simulation is excellent for integration purposes

12

With grateful thanks to

William Angwin and Madeleine Angwin

for all their help in the preparation and formatting of the drawings used in this Simulation

Printed in Poland
by Amazon Fulfillment
Poland Sp. z o.o., Wrocław